Love Stories

Poetry by

Norma
Beversdorf-Rezits

Anne Beversdorf,
Editor

Love Stories

Poetry by

Norma
Beversdorf-Rezits

Anne Beversdorf,
Editor

Stariel Press

Cover image: Norma and Thomas Beversdorf,
1950's. Family photograph

Back cover portrait, Norma Beversdorf-Rezits
in her 90's with her beloved second husband,
Joseph Rezits. Family photograph

This book is typeset in Bookman Old School
font.

Copyright © 2021
ISBN 978-0-9833930-3-0
Stariel Press

Stariel Press
Austin, Texas
www.stariel.com
StarielPress@stariel.com

Sharing the depth, honesty, and grace of Mom's love of people, the world, life – and the world beyond.

Contents

Preface

This is the third of a four-volume posthumous series of unrevealed poetry by my mother, Norma Beversdorf-Rezits.

These are poems of love, but not one is treacle. They speak of change, depth, her husband, children, pregnancy, and acceptance of foibles and loss. You will find subtle references to the death of her two-year-old daughter, to her autistic son (who wouldn't eat meat), and to her ability to maintain individuality in a long marriage to a complex artist. (He was a good and honorable man, but not an easy personality—we were all so glad when Joseph Rezits became her warmly supporting husband thirty-one years after my father's death.)

Some of Norma's poems have been set to music written by Lauren Bernofsky. You can hear them on YouTube by searching for *The Secret Philosopher.* The printed music can be obtained by contacting
Lauren Bernofsky at
lbernofsky@LaurenBernofsky.com.

Anne Beversdorf,
January, 2021

Norma Beversdorf-Rezits

i

Norma Beversdorf-Rezits: An Introduction

by
Anne Beversdorf

NBR's Poetic Work

Mom's poetry books have an unusual provenance. Because I was the only person who realized that Mom, Norma Beversdorf-Rezits, had been a serious poet her entire life, everyone else was surprised by the winter coat box full of poems discovered under her bed after her death.

The poetry in this collection was taken from several sources of Norma's carefully preserved works. These include

1. Her own curated diary compilation of several hundred poems gathered in 2004.
2. Three chapbooks of poetry given to her parents as holiday gifts
3. SEVEN folders of poems she gathered in groups in the winter coat box under her bed.

(I didn't dare explore the dozen-plus handwritten notebooks, mainly because her handwriting was known for illegibility!)

After receiving two beautiful poems from Mom in the early 2000's, I asked her if she'd kept the poetry she'd been writing all her life. She answered "Oh, yes!" When asked where, she answered "In a box under my bed." I asked if I could see them. And she answered "When I'm dead!" Which is what happened.

The poems in these volumes represent a small fraction of the approximately 700 poems Norma saved over her lifetime. If you knew her, you will think back to those occasions when she broke out of her good-humored, chatty manner and offered you a little glimpse of the soul who could write with such art and depth.

Biography

Norma Beversdorf-Rezits' life was both ordinary and unusual. Norma Beeson was born September 9, 1924, in San Antonio, Texas, an only child to loving parents. She received her BA in Music with a piano specialty from the University of Texas in Austin and married Thomas Beversdorf in 1945. Norma lived a conventional mid-century life as the wife of a classical music composer and professor, and as mother of their children.

Before maternity she taught music in the public school system in Texas. Later, she taught preschoolers and gave piano lessons to adults in Bloomington, Indiana, where Thomas Beversdorf was on the faculty at the Indiana University School of Music (now the Jacob School of Music). He became chair of both the Composition Department and the Brass Instruments Department.

Norma was known for her gracious charm and the numerous parties she gave celebrating her husband's music performances and honors. More privately, she had a sharp and often dry sense of humor that is sometimes evident in her poetry.

Norma's life and poetry were affected by more than just the events that most wives and mothers encountered in the mid-20th century. She had three daughters, the third of whom died at age two in an accidental drowning at home. She immediately had two more children, sons, the oldest of whom is profoundly autistic. He was born when few MDs in the world even knew what that was.

Norma rejected advice that he be placed in an institution, convinced she could "reach" him. Despite her son being non-verbal until age seven, she spent ten hours each day "training" him (literally saying "I didn't teach him. I trained him"). She made up her own methods, both supporting and making use of his strengths rather than trying to make his weaknesses reach traditional educational standards.

When her second son was born, Norma's husband invited both of her parents to move from Texas to Indiana on a piece of land he deeded to them. There they could live across the street from their daughter's family and their grandchildren.

Norma was an early practitioner of yoga, again privately, at home, and had three of her children by natural childbirth in the early 1960's. She was an avid reader of Paul Valery, Paul Tillich, Erich Fromm, Martin Buber, Soren Kierkegaard, Eric Hoffer, and

Thomas Merton. I was aware of her reading the poetry of T.S. Eliot, and e.e. cummings. I'm sure there were others.

Thomas Beversdorf died of asthma in 1981 when their sons were still in high school. Tom and Norma were both in their fifties at the time. Within a few years both of her parents also passed. When Tom died, Norma was working on her Master's Degree in Special Education. After his death and on the completion of her Master's degree she started teaching in a small town near Bloomington. When it became clear that the district neither cared about nor supported special education at a minimal legal level, Norma left that position.

Because of Norma's unprecedented efforts, her autistic son continued to defy expectations and earned a B.S. in computer science. Ultimately he would find a stable job as a government computer programmer and programming manager. Her second daughter is a retired Fine Arts Librarian from Avery Library, Columbia University. Her youngest son is an MD specializing in neurology. I am the oldest child, and I am a professional western and Vedic astrologer.

After her sons finished college Norma travelled all over the world and enjoyed gathering with friends at card games, dinners, concerts and plays. When she was in her early eighties she moved to Meadowood, a vital, university-related senior living center. There she met and fell in love with Joseph Rezits, who had been a colleague of her late husband, and whose deceased wife had given cello lessons to Norma's autistic son decades earlier. Joseph Rezits had been chairman of the Piano Department at the IU Music School and still performed regularly.

Norma and Joseph thrilled family and friends with their joyful marriage at 88 years of age. They both declared that this was "the love of my life." After seven years of love and mutual support, Joseph died in November of 2019 and Norma followed him in May of 2020.

The Poetry of Life

In Norma's poetry, complex ideas are expressed in minimal words. Almost none of her poems are over one page in length. Many are less than twenty words.

We see here a deeply spiritual and independent woman, outwardly living a life that conformed to the norms and expectations of the mid-20th century world but defining her own awareness and individuality in her private world of poetry. Her love of ambiguity, her unwillingness to label things Good or Bad, her ability to see universality in seemingly disparate views are all evident in her work.

It becomes obvious, in retrospect, that this work was a necessity for her strongly independent identity, and that her poetry is the work of her soul, writ small but powerfully, serving the needs of her deepest self.

This book of poetry offers a glimpse into Norma Beversdorf-Rezits' deep understanding of the complexity of love. Those of us who were recipients of her love received a priceless gift. We are glad to share it with you.

January 2021

Norma Beversdorf-Rezits

Love Stories

Norma Beversdorf-Rezits

Your dreams are mine
Not yours alone
To frame the earth
and heaven above –
Should once the dream
Together part, I'd
Be inclined to close
My eyes and wait
In depths where
First we met.

Norma Beversdorf-Rezits

I do not miss
You see,
those things
which are
a part of me.

The sky is there
to share with
all the earth,
and stillness
breathes a
quiet embrace
While people,
too,
become as one.

So pieces move
in rhythmic
symmetry,
and loving you
has come
a part of me.

Norma Beversdorf-Rezits

My love
You live
Because
You have
No
Precedent.

Norma Beversdorf-Rezits

Sometimes
you quietly fall
upon my face –
as from the sun
so lightly placed.
I cannot feel
your weight,
yet from
eternity
you come.

Norma Beversdorf-Rezits

What funny fuzz
is love
so sewn
intrinsically
becoming
one of twos
whose winning
was an Is
whose warming
glows and
overflows
and knows utmost,
kindling, infinitely.

Norma Beversdorf-Rezits

Norma Beversdorf-Rezits

I tickle you
with itchy toes
then fly to
hide before –
When slight
in pause
forgetting –
See, I am!

And so, so
far I'll be
aloft to
crawl my
ceiling
high, then
sleeping
light, while
letting days
homogenize.

Norma Beversdorf-Rezits

Wisdom's
Unquestionably
good.
Solomon
did well
by all
his wives.

Norma Beversdorf-Rezits

I've found
my
haven home.
A soul
within a soul
Not mine
but more my own
than mine –

I do not
own
a thing –
Not one
while
owned
myself
I
come.

Norma Beversdorf-Rezits

Ten thousand words
then random choose
just three –
a speciality –
tight sealed
hermetically;
No other ears
could hear
Let lips
just each
to speak
Then from the three
(avoiding wide
new range of
entities:, Have
nots, Do nots,
Say nots; become
a constant hum)
So we ho-hum to
Bleat our
Three

Norma Beversdorf-Rezits

Thank God
for pregnancy
a bloom so
full and
incomplete,
awaiting
(almost bursting)

Think not
of her
while he
so silently
rides
continual
creation
still aching
for birth

Norma Beversdorf-Rezits

Conception
Creates
A
Creature
Unknown
To
creator.
Acceptance
makes
love
a budding
necessity.

Norma Beversdorf-Rezits

Precious
growing
always
him
again
over
again

Norma Beversdorf-Rezits

Oh sweetness
dreams while
living more
as breathing
holds quiet
mystery in
twos

and knowing not
while
knowing all
unite in
quiet community

  Oh
she, by
his side
where bodies
need to
be, and
there
together
breathe
what seems
eternity

Norma Beversdorf-Rezits

Courage and cowardice
The same
Marital partners
Image and reflections
of another.

Norma Beversdorf-Rezits

Norma Beversdorf-Rezits

Work
as done
for the
beloved
is
blessed
before
begun.

Norma Beversdorf-Rezits

I love
To all
the
Extremes.

Extremes
Will adjust
If they
Must
and I, in honor
Obey.

Norma Beversdorf-Rezits

into
eternity

you pierce
me

squeezed

into
clutching
life's

equisite
needle's
eye

Norma Beversdorf-Rezits

So
   you feed
   incessantly
   touching
   light
   beyond
   the
   way

Norma Beversdorf-Rezits

Norma Beversdorf-Rezits

Sweet marriage
infinity
To be as
always me,
An instant
blessed As
all of life
upon a –
moment
rests.

Norma Beversdorf-Rezits

Norma Beversdorf-Rezits

Charred bodies float
still breathing air

The sky is deep
despair – then
shatter me

To grieve
is
disbelief.

Norma Beversdorf-Rezits

My thirst
exceeds
the birth's
release

Though
freed
I'm bound
Unleashed
by mounds
in tightest
scrutiny

Norma Beversdorf-Rezits

Because a leaf
plays with
a tree, still
holding lovingly,
the sun warms
shadows for
another yet
to be.

Norma Beversdorf-Rezits

I brand you
Today
So you
may run
and play –
Tomorrow
brings
a cut on
loins –
Ah feast
the dead
away.

(my vegetarian)

Norma Beversdorf-Rezits

Blessed orneriness
from you
spring
Thoughts malformed.

But
well nurtured
deformity
Might conceive
a
Creature
Unique
In
Beauty.

Norma Beversdorf-Rezits

Awake
sweet innocence
but do not die
awake,
sleep on again
until
and then
and then –

Oh
overtake
the fruited
tree
and hold a
portion free
to be, and be
forever
free –

Norma Beversdorf-Rezits

I hold her hand
And she holds mine
We drink the air
As one
And then she turns
To go her way
And I return
To mine.

Norma Beversdorf-Rezits

I see the
gentle ways
which
keep you
weaponless
with
distance
as
defense.

Norma Beversdorf-Rezits

I love, you
see, a film-
like delicacy
which opens
all while
veiling lends
a soft totality
and breeds a
new familiarity.

Norma Beversdorf-Rezits

Norma Beversdorf-Rezits

A breath enclosed
Can suffocate
A breath withheld
Can expiate –
So quicken life
My intimate.

Norma Beversdorf-Rezits

Bestow not on me
All your love.
Reserve a part
For another role
If but a glance
From your depth
Becomes my dream
Why have more?

Norma Beversdorf-Rezits

In me
You see
That known
Before.

Norma Beversdorf-Rezits

Perfume is sweet
But does not clean.
Then why do I cling
To the fragrance
Of words
When all
Reprisals
Have buried the bloom?

Norma Beversdorf-Rezits

Norma Beversdorf-Rezits

You've murdered me
too delicately
for all to see –
In streaming parts
dulled agony
relieves the sting
oblivion rings.

Norma Beversdorf-Rezits

Norma Beversdorf-Rezits

If, indeed
there is
So little
You demand
of me –
Then
turn inward,
please,
to see,
if how,
By the infancy
of sharing
We come
to be
a
pleasant
unity –

Norma Beversdorf-Rezits

Norma Beversdorf-Rezits

Would
You
Like
Me to
Hate –
Make it
Easy
To
Play
At a
Game
of
Deceit
or
Despair?

Norma Beversdorf-Rezits

Norma Beversdorf-Rezits

With gentleness
He never meant
To be aware
of base
Incongruities,
So himself
He removed
To find the
Darkness
Trailed
Behind.

Norma Beversdorf-Rezits

I cheat a corner
of myself
and see
corruption
in your eyes.
I hold a spark
in
beauty's light
releasing you,
my Paradise

Norma Beversdorf-Rezits

Norma Beversdorf-Rezits

You will I would
I do.
You think I should,
I do.
Your tale, believe,
I do
Your truth conceive,
Do I?

Norma Beversdorf-Rezits

I've you
Fixed
On a stick
Motionless
In pain.
Can you
See in my
Heart
Everything
And
Blame?

Norma Beversdorf-Rezits

Where love surrounds
Even
Its lowest ebb
Flows into eternity.

Norma Beversdorf-Rezits

Norma Beversdorf-Rezits

How nice
you are
and only
too
(unknowing)
Are as
you –

Norma Beversdorf-Rezits

You crash
my silent
reverie
and slash
the sounds
I cannot
bare, then
toss aside
immaculately.

How much
Can I
express
Yet still
allow
sweet mobility
to cradle
you?

Norma Beversdorf-Rezits

My ears
Can never hear
What my heart
Will not
Accept.

Norma Beversdorf-Rezits

Because
He won
Every
Battle
He lost
The war
Unknowing.

Norma Beversdorf-Rezits

Norma Beversdorf-Rezits

Could earth be
more than
you and me
Yet this
duality
I see
so constantly;
Upon this warmth
all others swarm
as on our peak
of silently.

Norma Beversdorf-Rezits

Norma Beversdorf-Rezits

I am afraid
the words
which are
might also
come
to err.

I hold so close
how could a line
define the most

Or yet, the worst,
(though I might try)
How could I lend a
single verb,
becoming then
your word.

Norma Beversdorf-Rezits

shadows grow
(and we between)
promoting tranquil
imagery – a
fleeting thing,
unruffled,
comes to be –

Norma Beversdorf-Rezits

Norma Beversdorf-Rezits

When you have said
up to your very edge,
Then circular come
in spiraling down
until you're found;
an island touching
shades – then you

Norma Beversdorf-Rezits

Norma Beversdorf-Rezits

.

To you – to me
a bounty (undescribed)
full of fortitude
to meet each moment
as it moves. Oh love
the lasting breath
of present death.

Norma Beversdorf-Rezits

Bloody bond of unity,
Cannot two hearts
Entwine with Beauty's
Streamers free, or must
The core be ugly sores
Blunt, scarred, unseen.

Norma Beversdorf-Rezits

If I were
In love
and not
with love
then why
be it love
to love
at all?

Norma Beversdorf-Rezits

Why should
You know
Your life
Transforms
a universe
if
All you are
is
All of you.

Norma Beversdorf-Rezits

Norma Beversdorf-Rezits

Why continue
Unpleasantries
When around
The horizon
Begins anew?
Why search
For a carbon
After "adieu"?
So simple
To ride
Uncomfortable ways,
But why,
Please,
Why Do
You?

Norma Beversdorf-Rezits

You move
Everywhere
Abundant
and free
Becoming
another to
another
another
and me.

Norma Beversdorf-Rezits

Because
In abundance
He gave,
She thought
He belonged
To her
Alone.
In stringent
Resentment
She shares
With a
World
Open
To his
Bidding.

Norma Beversdorf-Rezits

We share this cup
But wait to view
Another brew
Which seasons
For a spell
And pours into
Its thirsty hull.

Norma Beversdorf-Rezits

I called last night
But could you hear
When thunder rolled
And clouds were grey
Or is your life in tune
For light alone?

Norma Beversdorf-Rezits

Norma Beversdorf-Rezits

Now
He's mine
So now
Entwine
A heart
About my wrist
And dangle there
For all to view.
A favored one
Who favors me,
A femme fatale.
I'll not forget
And should he
Ever slide
I'll hold
My arm
Quite high
He won't forget
A chain.

Norma Beversdorf-Rezits

Imperious perversity
Confusion sweet
A madness
Undeclared
Wilt thou
Take
Wine or vinegar
My dear?

Norma Beversdorf-Rezits

I feel the strength
has drained
from me
yet
still
I breathe –
I am aware
that you
are there
and breathing
yes –
There is a new
totality
to give
new breath.

Norma Beversdorf-Rezits

How long
Can I
Maintain
Unending
Pleasure's
Pain?
As long
As hope
Creates
A force
To sway
Anew
Again.

Norma Beversdorf-Rezits

I cannot be
unless
I think as
I believe.
Sweet marriage
from
such
ecstasy,
blooms
radient fields
for
open arms.

Norma Beversdorf-Rezits

He has a need
To be, to be
Himself but
who was he –
He reached
and she, in need
received –
He still has need
to be, to be
while thinking
cynically.

Norma Beversdorf-Rezits

Still in my mind
Why call you
Mine – no more
than mine's the
sky above and
all the beauty
on the ground.

Still
In my mind
I'll call you
Mine
For mine's
the earth
the sky
and all
that I
Behold.

Norma Beversdorf-Rezits

Norma Beversdorf-Rezits

In
life a life is
spilling seeds
upon infinity –

Pretend – Yet
still you'll be
creating casts
upon each soul.

Norma Beversdorf-Rezits

Heap upon me
The burdens
of your pain
and holding
firm, seek
release again.

Norma Beversdorf-Rezits

Norma Beversdorf-Rezits

Incandescent
limbs
in morning light
illuminate the eyes,
By night, a
silhouette
in strength
of tenderness
Awakens every
nuance, kindling
incessantly –

Norma Beversdorf-Rezits

I live with you
Each day
And wonder what it is
To be alone;
Solitude's comfort
Togetherness a dream
Could anything, my dear
Make life more complete?

Norma Beversdorf-Rezits

Norma Beversdorf-Rezits

The scent
of love's
unknown
to one
who's framed
a beauty
there, so
on to one
quite strange
in ways
that gave –
Yet love
still strong
can
ache
beyond.

Norma Beversdorf-Rezits

Once
a dream ago
we
together spoke
no words
and were
within
a frame
unclaimed
by will
which
was not
real, yet
more a fact
than life
that's breathing
warm
to sun the soul
and fuel
eternity.

Norma Beversdorf-Rezits

I see you
Ride the
Atmosphere
and sweep
a path so
far away.
Then seen
Return
Awaiting
fuel to feel
the surge
which love
Creates.

Norma Beversdorf-Rezits

Norma Beversdorf-Rezits

If to
continue
you
cease
to be,
I
Comprehend
-
  unwillingly.

Norma Beversdorf-Rezits
145

Norma Beversdorf-Rezits

From a dream
It seemed a height
Unnamed, unseen
To have a love
So deeply know
The inner being
No marks could mar
An insight bare.

Then all too soon
It seemed a strange
New entity – the
Chains which came
From understanding
Greater than
Known before.

Norma Beversdorf-Rezits

Index of First Lines

Acknowledgments

Profound thanks to my sister, Paula Beversdorf Gabbard for cataloging and indexing Mom's poetry diary, seven folders and three chapbooks and for her aesthetic input. Thanks also to my brother-in-law Krin Gabbard for his brilliant rewrite of the back cover copy and for his enthusiasm and selection advice. Warm thanks to my friend Daniel Burton for his gentle and erudite editorial wisdom. Thanks again to my friends, Martha Ward and Karen Robison for their unflagging support and generosity. Knowing I have such skilled, thoughtful, and supportive friends contributed to the joy of this project.

The greatest acknowledgment of all goes to my mother, Norma Beversdorf-Rezits, who in addition to her secret poetry was a model for love, independence, intelligence, wisdom, and wit. We were lucky to have her.

Anne Beversdorf

Made in the USA
Coppell, TX
04 January 2022

70798900R00095